*Division of*

**DAYA PUBLISHING HOUSE**

**4760-61/23, Ansari Road,**
**Darya Ganj, New Delhi - 110 002**
**Phone: 23245578, 23244987; Fax: (011) 23260116**
**E-mail: info@regency-books.com**
**Website: www.regencybooks.com**



*ISBN 81-87498-40-4*

*Published by Regency Publications, 20/36-G, Old Market, West Patel Nagar, New Delhi 110 008 and printed at Radiant Printers, New Delhi, Phones: 574 0038, 571 2539; Telefax: 578 3571*

*Email: regency@satyam.net.in*

# Foreword

The North-Eastern Regional Centre of the ICSSR in 1991–92 decided to hold panel discussions in different parts of the region on the research priorities in Social Sciences in the area concerned. Consequently scholars and Department in the Universities of the region were indentified and a small amount of money was advanced to cover the estimated expenditure. Dr. S. Dutta, then Head, Department of History, Arunachal University, organised the panel discussion on November 3, 1992.

Dr. Dutta invited a number of scholars from the University and the colleges and the discussion was very well attended. Some of his friends and colleagues, namely A.C. Talukdar and S.N. Ali, both of the Department of Political Science, N.C. Roy, and Prabhat K. Pankaj of the Department of Economics, Tamo Mibang of the Department of History, Arunachal University and S.B. Chakrabarti of the Anthropological Survey of India, presented their papers at the discussion. Dr. Dutta later forwarded the papers together with his report to the NERC. We take this opportunity to thank Dr. Dutta and his colleagues not only for cooperating with the NERC but also for their painstaking efforts to help us in furthering the cause of Social Science Research in North-East India.

Somehow Research priorities of all the States in North-East India could not be completed to our satisfaction at the NERC. It was therefore decided to go through the papers and reports of the panel discussions and to publish them if found suitable. Experts were identified to go through the manuscripts and edit and update them. Research Priorities in Social Sciences in Arunachal Pradesh was entrusted to Dr. Gurudas Das of the St. Anthony's College, Shillong. Dr. Das has done his job well with single minded devotion and sincerity. We at the NERC thank him for all the pain that he has been taking on this account.

Arunachal Pradesh is one of the backward areas of the North-East. Most early works on Arunachal and its people were written by non-Arunachalees. Most of this work is also of a very high quality and has been done after considerable study and observation. In spite of the quality and quantity of the available work on Arunachal a lot more remains to be done, particularly in all areas of Social Sciences.

Shillong
July, 2001

Jai Prakash Singh
Ex. Hon. Director

# Preface

Social science research is a necessary precondition for any meaningful policy-making, for the management of society. Unfortunately, it has not yet been adequately treated so in our country. So far, very little attention has been paid to the development of an infrastructural network, to cater to the needs of the researchers. The results of many a work, which otherwise could have been used for the betterment of our society, have been either ignored or applauded without any serious note. Political expediency and ideological orthodoxy have played more important role in decision making rather than the results of objective enquiries. Not only the social scientists have been ignored in evolving the policies for social management, even the experience of the various social science disciplines are hardly utilized in advancing the cause of the society. In the era of globalization, however, performance of the state seems to have a pivotal role for the continuation of a government. And better state performance can only be ensured through closer contact between the social scientists and the policy-makers. The sooner such ties develop between these two, the better it is for the future of social science research.

I am thankful to ICSSR-NERC and its Deputy Director Dr. C.J. Thomas for giving me the opportunity to associate myself with this volume. I am also thankful to Dr. S.C. Daniel, Department of Philosophy, NEHU; Mr. N.K. Sarkar, Department of English, Shillong College and Dr. H.K. Srikanth, Department of Political Science, Assam University, for the help I received from them while editing this volume.

Gurudas Das

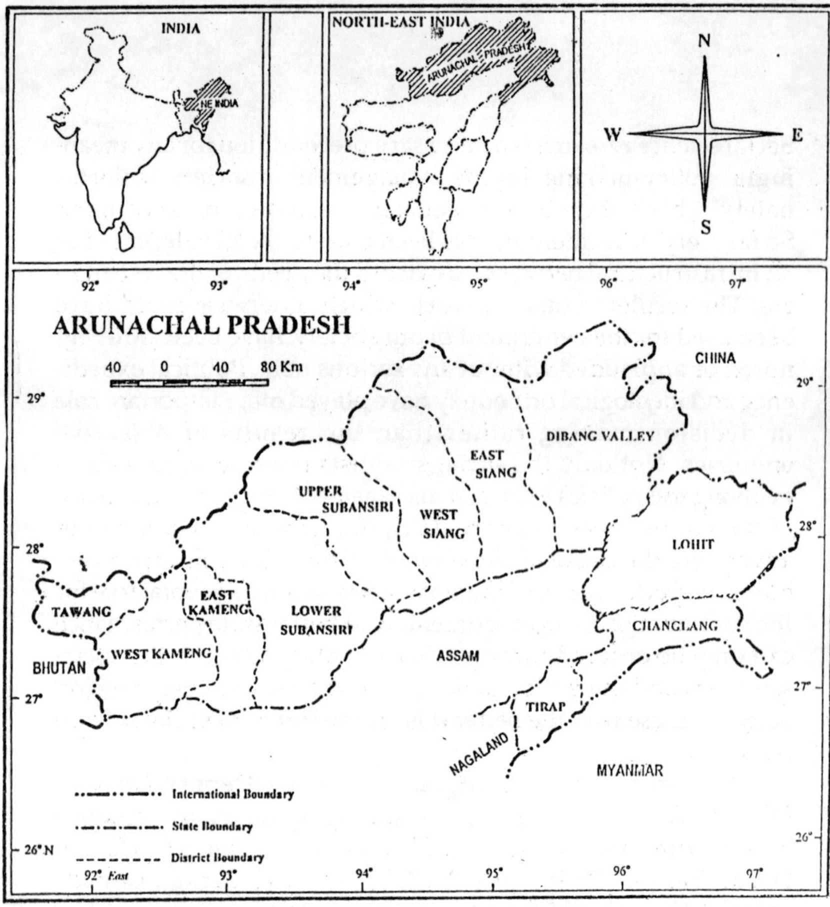
INDIA
NE INDIA
NORTH-EAST INDIA
ARUNACHAL PRADESH
N
W
E
S
ARUNACHAL PRADESH
40 0 40 80 Km
92°
93°
94°
95°
96°
97°
29°
28°
27°
26° N
92° East
CHINA
DIBANG VALLEY
EAST SIANG
UPPER SUBANSIRI
WEST SIANG
LOHIT
TAWANG
EAST KAMENG
LOWER SUBANSIRI
WEST KAMENG
BHUTAN
ASSAM
CHANGLANG
TIRAP
NAGALAND
MYANMAR
International Boundary
State Boundary
District Boundary

# Contents

# Contributors

1. A.C. Talukdar
Department of Political Science, Arunachal University, Doimukh, Itanagar, Arunachal Pradesh.
2. Gurudas Das
Department of Economics, St. Anthony's College, Shillong, Meghalaya.
3. N.C. Roy
Department of Economics, Arunachal University, Doimukh, Itanagar, Arunachal Pradesh.
4. Prabhat K. Pankaj
Department of Economics, Arunachal University, Doimukh, Itanagar, Arunachal Pradesh.
5. S.B. Chakrabarti
Anthropological Survey of India, Calcutta, West Bengal.
6. S.N. Ali
Department of Political Science, Arunachal University, Doimukh, Itanagar, Arunachal Pradesh.
7. Tamo Mibang
Department of History, Arunachal University, Doimukh, Itanagar, Arunachal Pradesh.

# Introduction

*Gurudas Das*

Following the industrial revolution in the West, the forces of social and political change became stronger. The urge for liberty, fraternity and equality had shaken many a society and built up pressure for social transformation. It is in this context that efforts began to develop the social science as a guide to social action since the beginning of the nineteenth century. Since then, it has been increasingly realized that if social change is to be controlled and directed towards a desired goal, the study of human being, *i.e.*, man to man relationship, human behaviour/action, man's relationship with his society, in sum, human reality as well as social reality—human conditions in the social environment in which he lives—only can provide the necessary knowledge which may come in use in organising and rationalizing social change.

The basic objective of social science, as it is widely held, is to study the social reality in a given society in order to find out the hidden laws that govern the social processes. In doing so, it analyses the functions of various social institutions, inter-institutional interactions and their inter-relationships that make the social structure. It may be reminded that social structure is the creation of man, and it is he who recreates it for his continuous search for betterment either through evolutionary or revolutionary change. In both cases, social science is supposed to act as a guide in identifying the social problems and suggesting measures for their solutions.

Now the question is: do we have one social science for the whole humanity? Or to put it differently: do all the social theories have universal applicability? If yes, then, is there any need to study each and every society since the results of study undertaken in one society can always be extended to all other societies. Unfortunately, in spite of the tall claims of universality by different social science disciplines, social realities differ from society to society and hence theorization of social phenomena in the context of one society cannot fully explain the social processes taking place in altogether different context.

Most of the modern social science disciplines like economics, sociology, political science, originated in the developed countries. Theories have been constructed in those disciplines in order to analyse the social reality of those countries. With the spread of modernization, these disciplines have been institutionalized in the university system. And with the spread of the university centred system of education in less developed countries, these disciplines have been introduced and theories are taught to the students which hardly explain the social realities that they confront with.

Of course, there is no denying of the fact that social theories developed in the West do provide clues to researchers in cognizing and identifying social processes elsewhere. But not to the extent as has been claimed by the universalists. Even the modernization theories which do not make any analytical difference between societies/nations also recognize that different societies/nations are passing through different stages of the common path towards modernization (Wallerstein: 1997). The prescription of ahistorical unilineal path towards modernity is a different issue which we do not intend to discuss here. What is important for us is to note the fact that as the different societies are at different stages of development, social realities in them also must be different which, in turn, reduces the universality claim of the social science theories. As a result, application of the same analytical framework to different societies in analysing the differential social realities in them may lead to different policy prescription. Here lies the need for society-specific social science research.

We shall now turn to the specific society, *i.e.,* Arunachalee society, with which we are concerned here, and argue first about the need for social science research on it, before prioritising the issues to be researched into.

## II
## NEED FOR SOCIAL SCIENCE RESEARCH ON ARUNACHAL PRADESH

Till the other day, Arunachal Pradesh was the "forgotten frontier" and the indigene therein were strangers even to many of the next door neighbours. It is only after independence that the name "Arunachal Pradesh" has been coined and the process of forging "Arunachalee" identity among the hitherto insulated tribal groups started. As the internal dynamics of social change within the tribal socio-economic formations was very weak, forces of change, through the programmes of modernization, have been thrusted externally by the state. In fact, the state is playing a crucial role as an agent of change.

For painless transformation from tradition to modernity, it is very important to know the traditional social environment, particularly as to how these communities attained equilibrium and ensured stability in the traditional system of governance, in order to handle the social, political and economic variables in favour of smooth transition. The scant knowledge about the social structure, asset structure, authority structure and their interaction that had led to socio-political stability in the traditional systems has been one of the major stumbling block for any effective intervention in accelerating social change in them. It is no better in case of designing a framework for change in material life. The areas of traditional skill formation among the people and their potentials in enhancing the material well being have not been explored fully without which it is difficult to design a ladder in the economic space as means to achieve the goals of modernity.

For the lack of relevant and policy oriented research, much of the efforts by the state in improving the conditions of human existence is not only yielding poor but often undesired results and thereby only adding to the frustration of the agents of change. Constant monitoring, identification of new processes, conceptualization of new variables for measuring the change which are essential and integral parts of a strategy of planned development are extremely lacking in Arunachal.

Thus, there is not only scope, but also urgent need, for social science research on Arunachal in order to understand the local specificities and identify the social, political and economic parameters which could be manoeuvred in improvising the policy matter for the smooth and speedy transformation of the idyllic communities from tradition to modernity. Besides, policy oriented research, there is also issues of utmost academic interest. As the historical isolation had, by and large, kept the tribal socio-economic formations away from outside influences, this situation provides us a unique opportunity to study the age-old social institutions which no longer exist in modern societies. This may enrich our understanding of the process of evolution of human society and culture and help in verifying our existing knowledge in the light of Arunachal experience.

## III
## TRENDS IN SOCIAL CHANGE: ASPECTS OF SOCIAL REALITY IN ARUNACHAL PRADESH

The processes of territorial incorporation of Arunachal hills as well as social integration of the tribal communities therein got momentum with the Independence of India. Functioning of these two processes have been captured in detail in one of my earlier works on Arunachal (Das: 1995). The Indian state has sought to integrate the area by extending the administrative paraphernalia as well as by superimposing the 'mainstream' political structure and process on Arunachal. Besides politico-administrative integration, economic integration has been attempted by allowing the market forces to penetrate as well as by gradual reshaping of tribal social and economic institutions in favour of market economy. The whole programme of social change initiated by the state is framed along the line of "modernization paradigm", the sweet coating name used to mean the capitalist path of development.

The sequence of planned change started with the so called Nehru-Elwin gradualist approach towards the integration of the hill tribes with national mainstream. Their protectionist-revivalist policy continued till the Indo-Chinese border conflict in 1962, and then, following the sharp criticism, it gave way to the policy of progressive integration (1964–1972), and finally the process of political integration reached to its culmination with the conferment of the status of Union Territory to Arunachal Pradesh in 1972. Subsequently, in 1987, it has been granted statehood.

In the early phase of modernizing programme, politico-administrative integration had received far more attention than the agenda for economic development. More emphasis was given to the creation of state structure, multi-tier political authority, introduction of modern political institutions, adult franchise, party line politics cutting across tribal boundaries, and to the establishment of the legitimacy of the new political order.

However, changes brought in the sphere of political structure and political process were not uncompromising and radical. The traditional authority structure had been accommodated in the new arrangement in order to avoid any possible conflict that could arise with the loss of authority of the traditional elites. Parliamentarian democratic structure had been superimposed without democratising/secularising the tribal values, ethos and culture. As a result, primordial values, the institution of tribe, clan and kinship had easily swallowed the political process frustrating the goal of modernization. All these have created a hybrid political culture where political behaviour of the majority of people is largely guided by tribe/ clan/kinship loyalty instead of higher social goals.

In spite of its failure to develop a democratic/secular political culture, the parliamentarian political structure has produced a class of power elites who are now locally acting as managers of the state and collaborating with their national counterparts. They mobilize people, and distribute the cramps of power on tribal lines, enjoy the status and privileges of high offices, make fortunes for themselves, but utterly lack in vision and foresight needed for society/nation building. Inapt in handling the intricacies of modern state, they are much depended on bureaucracy as far as planning the development and economic decision making are concerned. In the absence of any strong opposition, articulated pressure group, and media, the actual socio-economic agenda perceived by the different sections of people are hardly get translated into political decision making. As a result, the running of the affairs of state particularly in matters of development has largely become mechanical and rutinized in the sense of getting directives from the centre and making half hearted attempt to follow them without any improvisation.

In the sphere of economy, futile attempts have been made during the frontier phase (1947–1962) in order to revive and modernize the age-old tribal crafts. Although the area has been brought into the central planning process since inception, public investment remained very low till the fourth five year plan, ostensibly because of Nehru-Elwin protectionist and revivalist policy towards the integration of tribal communities with the national mainstream. The forces of capitalist penetration were not much encouraged by the administration. However, the whole perception has changed suddenly after 1962 border conflict. There has been a spurt in public investment on social overhead capital in order to open up the territory and subsequently push the administration inside Arunachal which was earlier operating from outside. The conferment of Union Territory status and subsequent administrative reorganisation had added further fillip in public investment. In the private sector, outside traders and entrepreneurs were allowed to operate in collaboration with their local tribal counterparts. In the absence of experienced local enterprising people who can carry on business in modern lines of production, the state also started playing the role of entrepreneur by entering into the areas of directly productive activities.

Following the huge investment made over the years in opening up the territory and creating the necessary infrastructure in the centres of administration—a number of urban agglomerates emerged which have been attracting gradual migration from rural areas. Developmental activities in later years have been largely concentrated in these urban enclaves. This has led to the emergence of a sharp rural-urban dichotomy in Arunachal economy.

The parliamentarian political structure has been instrumental to the power elites in cornering the direct benefits arising out of these developmental activities. Many of them have amassed a considerable fortunes by way of either working directly as contractors, sub-contractors, suppliers, etc., or indirectly by issuing permits, contract licences, supply orders to others against huge commissions and other forms of rents.

In the process a class of noveau-riche has emerged who subsequently have played a major role in exploiting the natural riches of the land in collaboration with regional and national capital. Within a short span of time, this has led to widening of inequality to such a great extent which was never before among the tribal communities of Arunachal Pradesh. Thus, the capitalist process of development has not only created spatial inequality, interacting with the political process has also generated social inequalities—both intra-community as well as inter-community—as the share of crumbs depends on one's proximity to power at the individual level, and in a number based political framework, on the numerical strength of a community.

The state, by investing on social overhead capital, has created an imbalance in Arunachal economy and then encouraged directly productive activities to grow under the private sector. It has extended various packages of incentives for the growth of both the agriculture and manufacturing sectors. The state policy towards modernization of traditional agriculture has emphasized a shift from jhuming to settled cultivation, diversification of crops, and development of horticulture and plantations particularly in the high hills in order to replace low yielding and eco-unfriendly jhuming. As the land development for wet rice cultivation requires sizeable investment on the part of the land-holders, government has offered a package of incentives. This policy has triggered the process of conversion of community land into private land and thereby shattered the age-old tribal economic organisation. The urban elites, those who could amass fortunes, have used this opportunity and strengthened their position further by way of investing in land. Some of them developed plantations in collaboration with the planters in Assam. This has reduced the size of the common property resources under the command of village councils and clan-bodies only to raise the level of deprivation of the rural commonfolk.

The emergence of private property in land coupled with adult franchise, modern education, urban life, modern health care have reduced the dependence of individual on traditional community institutions which have so long been playing a predominant role in protecting their members, providing them shelter and moulding their minds in favour of community life. The growth of individualism particularly in urban life has led to loosening the sacred primordial ties between a man and his primary group. This individuation—the process of emancipation of individual from sacred ties—albeit weak, has opened the way for new loyalties required for the changing society.

However, these trends of change are not uniform all over the socio-economic space of Arunachal. They are more pronounced in urban enclaves and relatively advanced communities compared to their rural and backward counterparts. Forces of modernization, being compromising for obvious reasons, could not dismantle the spatio-tribal boundaries, *i.e.*, claims of different tribes over the different parts of state's territory, in favour of inter-tribal as well as inter-clan use of land. Management of land is still done as per the customary laws which do not allow anyone else other than the members of same tribe/clan to own in its traditional habitat.

As a result, there exist sharp rigidities as far as factor mobility is concerned. Market forces have a very little role in allocating particularly the natural resources for their efficient use. The principle of market led efficient resource allocation maintained in the mainstream neo-classical economic theories is hardly applicable in Arunachalee economy. Tribal customary laws also restrict social mobility of the individuals and thereby weaken the forces of homogenization as well as the process of forging the "Arunachalee" identity. The customary laws in association with the Inner Line Regulations have also made the labour market insensitive to market forces. Indeed, the coexistence of tribal structures along with the modernizing framework has created a variety of multiple hybrid substructures all over the socio-economic space, which hardly lend themselves for generalisation.

Besides structural factor immobility, there is also market immobility—in the sense of price inelasticity of supply—of both factors and products because of high transport costs. The investment on social overhead capital has opened up vertical transportation channels between the hills of Arunachal and Assam plains at different points. As the north to south natural drainage system has made it very difficult for the construction of any cost-effective horizontal road transportation across the hills, no unified internal market could develop in Arunachal. As a result, the purchasing capacity of the Arunachalee society, whatever meagre it may be, does not produce any viable market signals for production to take place. Moreover, market mechanism does not help in levelling the price through movement of goods from surplus to deficit areas within the state. Both the factor and product markets of different parts of Arunachal are integrated with the adjacent plain areas of Assam. This segregated internal market has made the manufacturing of demand-based goods economically unviable even in the small scale sector. Besides this limitation arising out of small size of market, the programmes undertaken to modernize the manufacturing sector have also utterly failed to develop entrepreneurial skill among the local people through training and financial support. Entrepreneurship development programmes and schemes for financial support have essentially been viewed by the power elites as forms of privileges and have used them to please their kinsmen. Whatever resource based industries worth the name have come up, largely in the area of wood-processing, entrepreneurs from outside play the major role, while local tribals, in most cases, associate themselves as sleeping partners.

The failure of the modernization programmes in creating a space for non-agricultural activities in the economy particularly for the growing number of educated youths, who are waiting in the wings to join the labour force, has led to inter-tribal competition for state resources, *i.e.*, government jobs and other privileges. This inter-tribal competition for economic privileges in turn reinforce inter-tribal competition for political power. As the state is viewed as the source and distributor of privileges, the inter-tribal competition for power often leads to either shifting of group identities by the smaller groups between their numerically larger counterparts or claiming separate identity for themselves depending upon the suitability of circumstances as to which strategy will enhance the interest of the groups. The complex interaction between the electoral political process and the process of inter group competition very often leads to irrational allocation of resources compounded by considerations other than economic efficiency.

Thus the socio-political environment that has emerged in Arunachal Pradesh in the process of its integration with the national mainstream is now acting as a major deterrent to further economic development leading to perpetuation of its complete dependence on the central funds. The behaviour of the power elites in relation to shifting political loyalty in favour of party in power at the centre may largely be explained once this dependency syndrome is taken into consideration.

The social and political fallouts of this economic bankruptcy are often obfuscated by the political managers by playing one tribe against the other as well as so called "tribal solidarity" card against the non-tribals without addressing the real issues of rationalizing the social, political and economic processes in order to make them complementary and compatible to each other which only can strengthen the internal dynamics of change within the Arunachalee society.

## IV
## PRIORITIES IN SOCIAL SCIENCE RESEARCH IN THE TWENTY FIRST CENTURY

The trends in social change outlined in the preceding section indicate that the transitory phase—a spectrum between tradition and modernity—has just set in embracing Arunachalee society. And in a polar view of modernity, one may locate her nearer to the root. It may be noted that Arunachal experience hardly lends itself for explanation by the mainstream modernization theories. Here the processes of social change are not arising out of the internal dynamics of the society per se, rather because of state interventions. There are not many cases that have studied thoroughly by the theoreticians where the processes have been engineered by a state, which itself is passing through the transitional phase, that too in a part of its own, not integrated historically.

The research priorities in a society are largely ordered by the goals that the agents of social change set themselves. Of course, the goals set by the state, the main agent of social change, are not much different from the goals envisaged in the modernization paradigm except the fact that while the modernizing Indian state sees her image in western capitalist societies, it, in turn, strives to create its own image in areas which it seeks to integrate and modernize through intervention.

In the sphere of social processes the biggest challenge before the agents of change is as to how to forge " Arunachalee" identity out of multitudes of smaller tribal groups in order to provide stability to the present political structure in the long run. The present model that seeks to unify different isolated communities living within a politico-administrative boundary through their integration with the market network has largely failed to provide stable change and consequently has given birth to rising demand for territorial reorganisation and escalation of inter-ethnic conflicts particularly in the north-eastern region. In view of this experience, viable policy options need to be evolved in forging and cementing inter-tribal integration in Arunachal Pradesh.

In order to evolve alternative policy options for the accomplishment of this task, a huge amount of social investigations needs to be undertaken particularly in revealing the processes of fusion as well as fission that are working among the different tribal communities in Arunachal. It is also equally important to understand as to how resistances are being generated against the forces of homogenization and convergence due to the interactions between different processes of change—social, economic and political. Efforts in analysing and classifying these resistances may help in formulating/ reformulating the policies of directed social change.

It is important to evolve an intellectual space accommodating, by and large, the past social experiences of all communities for the growth of Arunachalee subnationalism. This calls for studies in micro-history including recording history of different groups from oral sources as well as recasting the ethnographic studies of the past in a comparative scale in order to arrive at a generalised common life-world of the past. The common past social reality, thus constructed, and properly disseminated through formal system of education, may act as a unifying force for the present and future generations.

In fact, we are facing a problem of double integration in relation to the people of Arunachal Pradesh. Firstly, integrating the different tribal communities with a larger territorial identity, *i.e.*, Arunachalee, and, then integrating it with the national mainstream. It needs to be rigorously analysed as to how the present model of integration working through a combined network of market, parliamentarian political structure and common lingua franca is serving these twin strategies in Arunachal Pradesh.

It is highly instructive to study the social ramifications of the penetration of the capitalist market forces into the tribal socio-economic formations in Arunachal. The emergence of private property in land has been instrumental in bringing a radical change in the relationships between man and man, man and society as well as man and environment. As a result, in some spheres the old relations of productions are gradually giving way to their newly emerged counterparts making them, by and large, similar to what exist in other societies in the country. The whole gamut of these changes need to be studied thoroughly in order to understand the nature and direction of social change that is taking place in Arunachal for effective intervention.

The nature of social change that is expected to follow from the programmes of modernization largely depends on the attitude, character, commitment and world-outlook of the elites—the change agents of a society. So it is important to study the attitude of the different categories of elites and their role in bringing the social change in Arunachal. In this context, it is of no less interest to assess as to what extent the various attributes of individualism like individual orientation and initiative, self mastery, ability to act alone, continuous striving for target set voluntarily by one-self, and faith in the efficiency of self-directed action, which are considered necessary for progress, have been acquired by these elites.

As the traditional social hierarchy based on status differentiation is gradually being replaced by class differentiation based on income and wealth, on the one hand, and interpersonal as well as inter-group co-operation by competition, on the other, it is highly instructive to study the process of class formation among, hitherto, less-unequal tribal communities of Arunachal Pradesh. An enquiry into the interconnections between the emerging class structure and traditional social hierarchy may be of great interest.

In the sphere of economy, the programmes of modernization seek to achieve self-sufficiency and development. In fact, development economics has been an offshoot of the modernization paradigm. Modernization of tradition bound societies has been viewed as a prerequisite for economic development. Modernity is conceived as the social, psychological framework, which facilitates the application of science to the process of production. And modernization, as Manning Nash puts it, "is the process of making societies, culture, and individuals receptive to growth of tested knowledge and its employment in the ordinary business of daily living" (Varma: 1980).

Following the launching of modernizing programmes and penetration of capitalist market forces, the equilibrium between philosophy, social and political organisations and productive system in the traditional communities of Arunachal Pradesh is gradually fading away. By introducing new political structure, inducing change in the productive system, and inculcating the philosophy of individualism, efforts are being made to change the social organisations so that the tribal communities can move to higher stages of development.

So far the change in productive system is concerned, the present model seeks to transform the shifting cultivation based subsistence tribal economy into peasant economy through the introduction of private property in land, wet rice cultivation, crop diversification, horticulture and plantation, on the one hand, and traditional crafts based manufacturing into modern industrial sector through encouraging the growth of industries in modern line of production, both under public and private sector, on the other. This model needs to be thoroughly reviewed. As the success of the model largely depends upon the creation of a strong interdependence between the two sectors, *i.e.,* agriculture and industry, it is important to study the pattern of sectoral linkage that has emerged in the process of planned development of the Arunachal economy. As the establishment of any leading demand based industry is not commercially viable due to the very small size of the local market, is there any justification for the adoption of such a two-sector developmental model in Arunachal Pradesh? A serious effort is needed to find out the alternative policy options for the development of an area like Arunachal, which has lately been integrated with the market network.

In the absence of any mature entrepreneurial class, since the state has been playing the role of an entrepreneur, it is important to evaluate the role of the state in creating the infrastructure and necessary institutional framework as well as providing policy framework for the growth of the manufacturing sector. The role of the state in initiating the process of industrialisation through direct participation also needs to be studied. Whatever industries have come up under public sector, the logic of public investment in them needs to be judged not only from cost-benefit point of view but also within the context of structural requirement of Arunachal economy as well as in terms of their opportunity costs.

In view of the non-viability of the growth of demand based industries, the development of resource based industries seems to be the other viable alternative. As a result, it is important to map out the availability of natural resources in the state and their commercial viability. As the high transport cost and infrastructural bottlenecks have made manufacturing non-competitive, it is important to identify the areas of comparative advantage that the state is having in relation to the national economy. It appears that Arunachal may have such advantages in the domain of resource intensive lines of production. More precisely, in lines of production for which necessary resources are available in Arunachal while they are scant in supply in other parts of the country. However, the establishment of resource based industries involves large investment and hence these could be developed either under public sector or in collaboration with outside private capital. In an era of liberalization, while the state is withdrawing itself from directly productive activities in favour of market forces and increasingly assuming the role of market manager, it seems to be unlikely that a policy of resource-based industrialization will succeed without the help of outside capital—national or multinational. In that case, it is important to delineate as to what policy framework is needed to attract outside investment in the state. In this context, it is immensely instructive to study the nature of contradictions between economic goals and social choices that most of the tribal societies in the north-east, including Arunachalees, are facing.

However, the degree of human development in a constituent state within a federal political structure may not always be reflective of its own economic structure. As the constituent states receive central funds under various schemes in order to provide basic needs like food, shelter, education and health, higher degree of human development is possible even when the structure of a state's economy indicates abject underdevelopment. Since out of every rupee spent by Arunachal government ninety paisa comes from the centre, it is important to assess the achievements of the state in providing the basic human needs to the people.

There are a number of indices developed by the social scientists in order to measure the extent of modernization/ development of a society. Different agencies and individual scholars have developed different indices on the basis of different sets of social, political, economic and demographic parameters. However, the important among the multitudes of variables used to measure the degree of modernization/development are: per capita income, per capita consumption of necessities as well as infrastructural inputs, savings, investible capital, rate of investment, productivity in agriculture and manufacturing sector, extent of monetization, availability of credit, development of financial institutions, rate of unemployment, size of labour force engaged in different sectors of an economy, extent of urbanization, extent of dualism, character of basic social organisation, extent of skill formation, literacy rate, infant mortality rate, life expectancy, etc.

These variables no doubt capture the strength and resilience of the structure of an economy. But the economic variables like per capita income, savings, investment, credit, and finance have meaning only in so far as there is a well-developed market system and high monetization of the production and distribution of goods and services in a society. The Arunachal economy which has not yet been fully monetized, where different sectors have not yet been integrated with the market system, where sectoral linkages are very weak, where individual's decision either as producer or consumer is largely guided by traditional values instead of so called "rationality postulate" of mainstream neo-classical theories—formal economic theories alone will hardly be instrumental in understanding, analysing and explaining the economic reality. It may be reminded that a formal view of economy can well explain the economic processes of the industrial societies as well as societies which have been fully integrated with the capitalist system. But this view cannot fully grasp the economic processes in a society where economic variables are, by and large, insensitive to market forces. In Arunachal, still the economic process is largely embedded in social and political processes. As a result, a substantive view of Arunachal economy seems to be more revealing than its formal counterparts.

It is also important to adopt an analytical view in explaining the material life process in Arunachal society besides empirical measurement of economic variables that gauge the degree of development/modernity. The empirical research which often adopts a comparative method, like mainstream development theories, hardly takes historical contextuality into consideration, and hence involves a great danger of misreading the social reality leading to erroneous prioritisation of social goals as well as irrational ordering of social claims. This is particularly important for empirical research on societies like Arunachal, which have lately been incorporated into and integrated with the national mainstream. As a result, besides comparative approach, researchers, while measuring the social and economic variables in such societies, should also adopt a diachronic view—that measures social change on a termoral scale—for the proper location of social reality.

In both cases—comparative and diachronic—research must be based on good quality data. The data used by most of the researchers working on Arunachalee society are largely drawn from official publications. Various government agencies collect them for specific purposes, in frameworks, forms and levels of aggregation which often not only fails to capture new processes even sometimes these are inadequate for scientific enquiry of social and economic phenomena. As a result, researchers on Arunachal Pradesh need to identify new processes, conceptualize new variables, and collect, store and analyse statistical data over time. Although it is difficult and highly expensive but is the only way to improve the observational and monitoring capabilities necessary for social sciences to be relevant for policy making and evaluation. In order to do this, efforts should be made to institutionalize social science research in Arunachal by way of establishing research organisations in different areas of enquiry. As the different processes of change—social, economic, political—are largely embedded in the material life process, the researchers may have to go beyond the conventional domain of social sciences in order to capture the social reality in Arunachalee society.

## REFERENCES

Das, Gurudas, 1995, *Tribes of Arunachal Pradesh in Transition*, Vikas, New Delhi.

Verma, Baidya Nath, 1980, The Sociology and Politics of Development: A Theoretical Study, RKP, London.

Wallerstein, Immanuel, et al., 1997, Open the Social Sciences: Report of the Gulbenkian Commission on the Restructuring of the Social Sciences, Vistaar, New Delhi.

CHAPTER 1

# Research Priorities on Social/ Cultural Anthropology

*S.B. Chakrabarti*

Social research is a special kind of involvement in quest of knowledge where causalities are attempted to be established on the recurrent and varied set of social phenomena. Once the relation between two or more sets of facts are identified, some kind of predictions are possible to make towards the trends of changes between these facts. The question of priority is dependent on very many individual, institutional, social, political and economic criteria. It is not the question of convenience of handling a priority, but it is also to be worked out in terms of socio-economic and politico-historical cost-benefit paradigm. Considering the great limitation of our resources—both human and financial—we must try to reduce the hangover by minimising duplication of work at the first instance and then making the result of our research immediately available for public consumption so that useful application of the same, if any, may be made in the larger interest of all concerned.

Logically it follows that we should have a proper documentation of what has already been done. Next we should identify the obvious gaps in information that need to be filled either by computing data from the available secondary source or by generating fresh data at the primary level by way of undertaking field research at the appropriate context.

So far social/cultural anthropology is concerned, we have quite a lot of information on the people of Arunachal

Pradesh mainly generated by the decadal census reports. The Directorate of Research, Arunachal Pradesh has also conducted a number of ethnographic field studies on various human groups of Arunachal Pradesh. Recently Anthropological Survey of India has done an extensive field study entitled People of India where a profile of the various communities of Arunachal Pradesh has been depicted. The result of the same will be ready and will be soon available in printed form. A thorough documentation of the coverage is now necessary in terms of plotting them in map superimposing all kinds of interrelated data and then comparing them for the purpose of meaningful generalisation. The analysis of census data of 1981 for Arunachal Pradesh including the census atlas may be a beginning in this direction where a whole range of socio-economic and cultural context may be compared. This task will be best achieved if attempts are made on evolving inter-disciplinary approach of all social science disciplines. A modest attempt of compiling bibliographical information on social science researches and publications has been made by the North-Eastern Regional Centre Shillong of ICSSR. Further efforts may be made for preparing the annotated bibliography in this line.

Even a cursory glance at the publications of the Directorate of Research, Arunachal Pradesh, would show that they have covered about forty ethnographic monographs on various major and minor tribal groups of Arunachal Pradesh. They have also published linguistic studies on about twenty-five tribal groups. This apart some special topics have also been published by them. It covers a large spectrum of the subject. To cite examples—*Philosophy of NEFA* by Verrier Elwin; Culture and Custom of Arunachal Pradesh, festivals of Subansiri and Kameng; religion among the Adi, Monpa, Sherdukpen and Singpho; Study of Tawang monastery; myth of Shinongs; dances of Arunachal Pradesh; love songs of Wanchoo and Nocte; handicrafts of Arunachal Pradesh; customary law of Arunachal Pradesh; Social organisation of the Minyong; musical instruments of the Adi, folksongs of the Wanchoo and so on. These publications also include District Gazetteers of Lohit, Tirap and Subansiri districts on the one hand and bibliography of books, notes and articles on Arunachal Pradesh on the other.

If one does a scanning of these materials some unidentified tribal groups, areas and some relatively uncovered issues would obviously emerge from them. To take a few examples, the tribal groups like Zakharings of upper reaches of Lohit Valley are less studied. The relatively isolated villages are less covered. The most important question of ownership and management of land in general has got scanty attention. The peculiar problem of the existence of a system of bonded labour among the Sulung has perhaps escaped our attention and so on and so forth. At the level of cultural history the social interactions in Parasuram Kund in lower reaches of Lohit river, the sacred heritage of Bhismakanagar in Dibang Valley, the historical relic of its fort at Itanagar may also be taken up for a detailed study. The political institutions like the *Kabang* among the Adi, *Ngonothum* among the Nocte, *Jong* among the Sherdukpen, *Mele* among the Aka, *Duliang* among the Apa Tanis, *Wancho-Wancsa* among the Wanchoo may be studied at a comparative level. The ideological input for the believers in Buddhism and the indigenous magico-religious faith as well as the emerging Christianity at certain pockets may be taken up for in-depth investigation by way of defining and delimiting a cultural boundary among various groups as well as cultural continuum across the regions. A typology of belief systems and its impact on the mutual interaction among the groups of people may evolve out of this enquiry. The impact of Donyi-Poloism and its missionary activities and its influence on the people may also be studied in the actual context. The study on the available script is another area of useful research. The study of human adaptation in extreme climate is also very important aspect of research in this region.

The whole of this country in general and the north-east Indian States in particular are passing through some stages of transformation. While there are a common idiom of macro factors for all of them like the technological development, the monetized economy, the international network of trade and commerce, the overall bureaucratization of political and educational processes, the increasing trend for a higher rate of consumerism, etc., north-east India including Arunachal Pradesh is also known for having its own unique situations. For example, the relatively formidable landscape, the apparent community based system of sharing the resources, the geographical isolation and its placement in the context of a number of international boundaries, the relatively lesser exposure to technological advancement, the constitutional safeguards for various security measures, etc., have also contributed in their own way for the retention of some traditional social base on the one hand and to interact with the larger communities by way of participation in a uniform national, political, economic and administrative framework. The regional peculiarities at work do not negate the plural societies and cultures of Arunachal Pradesh from undergoing the historical trend of newer social formations and its consequential transformations. Obviously we are naturally confronted with the problems of growing ethnic consciousness and its manifestation in corporate community life on the one hand and the emerging problems of development at the cost of erosion of old moral values on the other. A lot of conflicts and contradictions emanate between the formulations and implementations of the development projects. Research studies are very much necessary on each of these issues just mentioned. The 21st century would probably face a number of alternative options. These will get effective feed back provided we get to know the intricate mechanism of controlling social, political, economic and cultural processes that keep the societies going from one level of consciousness to the other. In order to have first hand knowledge about such processes and the systems (which is otherwise known as the people's perception) one has to fall back upon the rigorous research material that would provide the solid intellectual base for tackling such issues. At this stage this approach also calls for the research projects with applied bearing.

CHAPTER 2

# Challenges of Development

*Prabhat K. Pankaj*

**Introduction**

The economy of Arunachal Pradesh is varied in composition. Heterogeneity is the single most feature of this region. The existing heterogeneity has more to do with its historical background, anthropological lineage and existing practices than to a mere quantification of development variables. With areas increasingly being covered under money-market, Arunachal Pradesh has acquired a new face of its own. The "barter-economy" is gradually giving way to "money economy". The State is passing through a transition phase of economic development.

The government has assumed the role of development agency in the state. Programmes have been chalked out and implemented. It has produced some desirable effect. Expansion of service sector has been successful in creating jobs. The living standard has gone up. The general health and education level have been pushed up. Roads have been constructed and social overheads created.

Nevertheless, there have been several anti-developments seen around. The overall growth of income has not been evenly distributed. Inequality of income, wealth and opportunities have been rampant. Ever increasing population coupled with the growth of educational institutions have increased the volume of educated unemployed in the state. Agriculture has come under tremendous pressure with more and more population added towards it. A gradual shift of population with ample "crowding out" has been visualised from rural agricultural sector to urban service sector. The expansion of medical services have been far less than satisfactory. Deforestation has started posing a threat to environmental degradation. Housing the people in a proper way remains a formidable task. The government seems lacking a long term plan. The 21st century is likely to be crucial for providing a proper direction to the economy of Arunachal Pradesh and to put it on the path of "sustainable development".

The present paper is an attempt to identify the growth connections in the state which would meet the challenges of development in the times to come. The focus is on the priority areas and the associated research priorities in the 21st century.

## Agriculture and Industry

Agriculture has been left to private sector in the State. Land has been the centre of economic activity. The type of agriculture pursued has been known as shifting or slash-and-burn cultivation. The type of activity found in this sphere has been land cultivation after removing the jungle through burning and cutting; fishing; hunting; and food gathering. These activities together constitute the main source of livelihood of a majority of scheduled tribe population.

Among the items produced in agriculture sector are rice, wheat, maize, millets, pulses, mustard, groundnut, soyabean, etc. There has been a great variation in the yield of agricultural commodities produced (Appendix: Table I). The variation is found to be the maximum in case of groundnut followed by soyabean, wheat, mustard and millets. It is the least in case of maize, rice and pulses. This provides a basis for the identification of higher productivity area for a particular commodity (Appendix: Table II).

By and large the income elasticity of demand for food is still positive. The fact that the co-operative societies are engaged, more in bringing foodgrains from neighbouring states than to procure them from inside at conducive price, is enough commentary on the present state of food production. The absence of government off the farm has neither been conducive to enhance agricultural output nor been able to protect the peasant, specially those who have made a switch over from foodgatherer to peasantry. The co-operative societies have to play a vital role in bringing agriculture into the realm of market through their traditional mode of functioning. For this, a comprehensive plan for their spread and smiothening is required.

The existing land use pattern gives enough indication of the lack of proper land planning for cultivation purpose. A vast chunk of land is still unutilized. The percentage of net area shown is less than the percentage of land not under cultivation including fallow land to total area under operation. The ratio stands at 43:57. The land not under cultivation excluding fallow land to total area under operation is 35%. It includes—(i) land put to non-agricultural usage, (ii) barren and uncultivable land, (iii) permanent pastures and other grazing lands, (iv) culturable wastes and (v) land under miscellaneous tree crops and groves. The culturable wastes alone constitute 61% of other uncultivable land excluding fallow.

Ample scope for horticulture exists in the state. The production of temperate, tropical and sub-tropical fruits have been quite impressive, though the average yield has gone down over the years 1987–88 to 1989–90 (Appendix: Table III).

Commercialisation of fishing practices, *i.e.*, the spread of pisciculture will be one of the most viable income generating activity in the state. There is a big case for poultry development as well. If fishing and poultry can be developed in rural and urban areas respectively, it will become a sustainable source of income, employment and savings.

There has been very little dairy activity in the state. It is high time to realise its importance. The demand for milk is on higher side. To begin with, Government may start a few dairies in townships keeping their population into account. It can purchase cows and buffaloes from states like Punjab and Haryana and get the milk distributed on profit basis. It will generate surplus in the hands of the government which can be utilized for some developmental purpose and through gainful employment, income will be generated in the hands of the common people. In the later phase, some units to produce milk products, can also be established.

There has to have a well established interconnection between agriculture and industry in the state. The problem of unemployment, income generation, saving mobilisation and raising the general living standard cannot be solved unless the two sectors, agriculture and industry, reinforce each other. It has to be agro-based industry under government sector. It will generate demand for agricultural products and hence will ensure against their prices to collapse. There will be a shift of labour force towards industries from agriculture and other activities.

The present endeavour of "Controlled Spread" of the SSIs by the government is likely to create growth imbalances in the state. Firstly, the units are mostly located at the urban centre and secondly, it has been instrumental in generating income in those hands which already have a minimum envisaged purchasing power. However due to a host of technical and institutional factors, these units have not been able to generate any growth impulses.

A selective list of industries based on local product and "the state of art technology", e.g., craft, garments, etc. should be prepared for providing loans. Electronic items should also be included into it. These units should be earmarked for preferential treatment. The units are to be location based. The manufacturing activity should be taken up by the Government on medium and large scale.

**Education and Employment**

The spread of primary and higher secondary education needs to be ensured. The higher educational institutions, colleges and University, have to ensure quality education otherwise we are likely to have a vast army of educated unemployed in the state. It would be important to see whether the benefits of higher education are getting confined only to higher income groups or are working as tools to ensure an egalitarian society. An equal access to education for people belonging to different economic classes has to be ensured.

The available data on employment situation are quite insufficient as it does not include the major category of selfemployed people in the state. As per an estimate, out of every 10 jobs created in the state, 9 are self-endeavoured. The existing trend on "main workers", "marginal workers", and "non-workers" is shown in Table IV (Appendix). The trend shows (i) the dominance of male workers in "main workers" category, (ii) females are widely employed as marginal workers and (iii) females are proportionately more unemployed than their male counterparts. If we look at the statistics relating to "sex ratio shift" and the "age composition of employed population" and relate it to above observation, it would be possible to draw some interesting inferences. There has been no change in the sex ratio in between 1971 and 1981. It was 861 in 1971 and 862 in 1981. The rural sex ratio stood at 881 in between 1971 and 1981. The urban scene has witnessed a huge change. It became 628 in 1981 from 457 in 1971.

There are 39.43 percent population under 0–14 age groups. The age structure of working population shows an extraordinary concentration under 35–59 age group. The percentage of population under the age groups 15–34 and 15–59 are 32.93 and 55.81 respectively. The age group 35–59 alone constitutes 22.88 percent population. Only 4.76 percent population are under 60 + age group.

The inferences that we could draw are, (i) "main workers" are mainly 35–59 age group people. They are the people who got into the government jobs some 10–15 years ago. The organized sector has not expanded to the extent that the new youngsters could be absorbed fully, (ii) a sheer lack of industrial sector coupled with stagnating service sector is likely to be the root cause of massive educated unemployment in the state, and (iii) the urban female population has not been able to get into the "main workers" category to the desired extent. They have been rather relegated to "marginal workers". The bias against fair sex in gainful employment is quite visible.

## Energy and Infrastructure

The state has immense scope of power generation. It can serve as a native industry by itself. This "universal intermediary" will be in high demand in the years to come. It is going to be a crucial infrastructure for the development of the region because, it can be transmitted over long distances and in remote areas. The state has the potentiality in thermal energy, geo-thermal energy, wind power and hydro-electricity.

The Government has to shoulder the responsibility of building a network of infrastructure and other social-overhead capital. The policy to be pursued in this regard should be to take the infrastructure to the place where people are.

In the wake of ever growing population and the related issue of their living standard, the housing demand will be on higher side. A comprehensive housing survey is required to assess the present standard and future demand. An "indicative planning" for housing as a part of the composite development scheme is called for.

## Research Priorities

In the field of agriculture, research projects can be taken up on (i) land use pattern and the changing production relationship; (ii) land productivity and regional production disparity; (iii) the extension and the spread of horticulture, sericulture, pisciculture, dairy and poultry, and (iv) programme evaluation studies. Techno-economic surveys of various regions should be planned to assess the needs and potentialities of respective regions. Feasibility surveys with regard to (i) food processing industries, (ii) agro-based industries, (iii) dairy, fisheries and poultry and (iv) village handicrafts and cottage industries, (v) ancillary and feeder industries and (vi) readymade garment manufacturing industries, should also be taken up on priority basis. An individual research project can be taken up to study the socio-economic impact of the spread of education, both primary and higher, in the state. Their respective rate of returns in terms of Government subsidy and job accessibility can also be calculated.

A socio-economic survey of women's status in the State is another area of research. The Government can take up a technical study to find out the scope of power generation in the state. A comprehensive housing survey is required. This can be taken up by voluntary organisation in liaison with other organisations or by the government itself. Micro-level study by individual researcher should also be taken up. Programme evaluation study by individual researcher or by an organisation is always called for.

## APPENDICES

**Table I: Variation in the Yield of Agricultural Commodities, 1989–90**

| Commodity | Standard Deviation of yield among 11 districts in % | Mean yield in % | Co-efficient of Variation in % |
|---|---|---|---|
| Rice | 1.70 | 11.88 | 14.31 |
| Maize | 0.61 | 12.25 | 05.01 |
| Wheat | 3.47 | 16.18 | 21.42 |
| Millets | 1.64 | 09.24 | 17.74 |
| Pulses | 1.12 | 07.76 | 14.41 |
| Groundnut | 4.53 | 12.18 | 37.21 |
| Soyabean | 4.13 | 13.35 | 30.97 |
| Mustard | 1.37 | 07.67 | 17.82 |

Calculated upon the data available in the *Statistical Abstract of Arunachal Pradesh,* 1990, DES, Government of Arunachal Pradesh, Shillong, pp. 21–23.

**Table II: Higher Agricultural Productivity Area, 1989–1990**

| Commodity | Districts |
|---|---|
| Rice | AEP |
| Maize | AEP |
| Wheat | Tawang, East Kameng, Lower Subansiri, Tirap, East Siang and Lohit |
| Millets | Tawang, Lohit, East Kameng, and Subansiri |
| Pulses | AEP |
| Mustard | West Kameng, Lohit, Dibang Valley, Tirap and Lower Subansiri |
| Groundnut | Lower Subansiri, Tirap, West Siang and Upper Subansiri |
| Soyabean | Lower Subansiri, East Kameng, Tirap and Dibang Valley |

AEP: Almost Equal Productivity.

**Table III: Average Yield of Fruits Production**

| Sl. No. | Fruits | 1987–1988 | 1989–1990 |
|---|---|---|---|
| | **A. Temperate** | | |
| 1. | Apple | 1.18 | 1.63 |
| 2. | Pears | 2.75 | 1.93 |
| 3. | Plum | 2.31 | 2.16 |
| 4. | Walnut | 0.07 | 0.07 |
| 5. | Peach | 2.25 | 2.21 |
| | Average | 1.84 | 1.82 |
| | **B. Sub-tropical/tropical** | | |
| 1. | Gauva | 1.45 | 1.43 |
| 2. | Banana | 5.92 | 1.55 |
| 3. | Pine Apple | 4.76 | 4.31 |
| 4. | Orange | 1.98 | 1.58 |
| 5. | Papaya | 1.79 | 1.73 |
| | Average | 3.18 | 2.12 |

Calculated upon the data available in the "Statistical Abstract of Arunachal Pradesh, 1990", DES. Government of Arunachal Pradesh, Shillong, p. 27.

**Table IV: Employment Pattern 1981**

| S. No. | Workers | Ratio | |
|---|---|---|---|
| 1. | Total workers to total population | 0.53 | |
| | (i) Main-workers to total population | 0.50 | |
| | (ii) Marginal-workers to total population | 0.03 | |
| 2. | Male to female population in "Main-workers" | 1.64 | (M:62.16 F: 37.84)* |
| 3. | Male to female population in "Marginal-workers" | 0.28 | (M:21.57 F: 78.43)* |
| 4. | Male to female population in "non-workers" | 0.88 | (M:46.90 F: 53.10)* |

Calculated upon the data available in the *Statistical Abstract of Arunachal Pradesh*, 1990, pp: 4–5.

* Percentage of Male (M) and female (F) to total Main-workers, Marginal Workers and Non-workers respectively.

CHAPTER 3

# Political Science: Some Priority Areas in Research

*A.C. Talukdar*

## Introduction

Political Science is a Social Science and so Political Science research is essentially a Social Science research. What is a Social Science research? Stated briefly, a social science research is a pursuit of knowledge about human behaviour, for its own sake as well as for the sake of the betterment of human destiny. In the former case it is called a pure or basic research and in the later case it is called applied or practical research. Pauline V. Young, in her work "Scientific Social Surveys and Research" defines Social Science research as a "Scientific undertaking which by means of logical and systematic techniques aim to discover new social facts or verify and test old facts." It also attempts to develop new scientific tools and new concepts and theories which would facilitate reliable and valid studies of human behaviour. Thus, the aim of social research is to explore and gain proper understanding of human behaviour and social life. This understanding further helps us to gain a greater control on human behaviour and social life. Social Research therefore, can be defined as a systematic method of explaining, analysing and conceptualising social life in order to extend, correct or verify existing knowledge.

Contemporary Political Scientists have realised that political behaviour of the people in a given society can be studied and understood only in the context of the whole system. Political behaviour is quite unintelligible in the framework of a set of legal rules and institutions. In order to understand a political phenomena it must be studied in the context of the entire social order manifesting in one of its many dimensions. It is because of this, today the political scientists have realised that Political Science has been increasingly enriched by economic, social, psychological, anthropological, historical, statistical and geo-political data which are of equal relevance to political science. Thus Political Science research today more often than not is an interdisciplinary study. The interdisciplinary and system approach also emphasises on more and more empirical studies. Of course, the facts gathered through empirical studies will have to analyse in reference to a theoretical framework, for facts and their relationship can hardly be understood without a theoretical frame of reference. Prof. Iqbal Narayan, one of the eminent political scientists of the country, while addressing a symposium on "Inter disciplinary approach to the study of Folklore" in 1990 at Shillong emphasised the point that Social Scientists like the historians, sociologists, anthropologists, economists, political scientists folklorists and others should turn to each other while studying the society and the process of change particularly in the North-Eastern Region. Nothing can be more true to Arunachal Pradesh. We shall do well to bear in mind this, while talking about priority areas of research in political science in Arunachal Pradesh or for that matter in any other Social Science.

## Status of Political Science Research in Arunachal Pradesh

Of late the North-Eastern Region, owing mainly to political reasons, has attracted the attention of many scholars and researchers and a number of studies have been carried on the Region. Some of them relate to Arunachal Pradesh. But inspite of the existence of a number of funding agencies such as the UGC, the ICSSR, the ICHR, the Anthropoligical Survey of India, NEC, the Agro-Economic Research Centre, and the Research Directorates of the State Government today, Social Science research, including political science research on Arunachal Pradesh is far from satisfactory.

During the British period certain academically oriented civil servants wrote certain accounts of some tribes in Arunachal Pradesh. After the independence also this trend was followed to some extent. Verrier Elwin, Heimendorf, J.N. Chowdhury, L.N. Chakrabarty, P.N. Luthra, Sachin Roy, Y.A. Raikar, Ligin Bomjen, P.C. Dutta, T.K. Bhattacharjee are some of the scholars who carried such studies about the tribes of Arunachal Pradesh. Some of their works contain reference to socio-political life of the tribes they dealt with. Verrier Elwin conducted a comprehensive study of the political institution of the tribes of Arunachal Pradesh in his *Democracy in NEFA* in 1969, P.D. Gogoi did his Ph.D. work on *NEFA Local Polity*, but the thesis is not yet published. On the other hand the Research Department of Arunachal Pradesh has published more than a hundred works. They include 53 anthropological-sociological books, 29 historical language books, 6 archaeological books and 3 district gazetteers. The rest are unpriced books and pamphlets including at least 3 of them titled *Research in Arunachal Pradesh*. But most of them are monographs which depict the tribes in their pre-contact days. So, they can serve at best as the benchmark data for further research work. Very few social scientists have undertaken specialised topics like political development, social change, process of modernisation, emerging pattern of leadership or social differentiation etc. However, in last one decade or so a few empirical studies have been carried out on socio-political process in Arunachal Pradesh by scholars like B.B. Pandey, Bijon Mahanta, Sanjey Dubey, Nari Rustomji, Jogoda Phukan and the present author. However most of them are micro level studies. But it goes without saying that if socio-political behaviour of a group is to be clearly understood such studies must be fruitfully linked to the macro level study of the society, showing its relationship to the entire society. According to a study carried out by Goswami and Phukan, Arunachal's share of social science research even among the North-Eastern States is only 12.4%. Of course, in recent times a number of research papers have been published in various journals of the country. The lion's share being in the three journals—*NEFA Information, Arunachal News* and *Research* all published from Arunachal Pradesh. Sipra

Sen, has brought out a comprehensive bibliography (*Arunachal Pradesh and the Tribes*, 1986, Gian Publishing House New Delhi) wherein she has listed a total of 2073 titles of books, papers and pamphlets on Arunachal Pradesh. However, very few of them can be called socio-political studies (not more than 150 titles of books, papers and pamphlets all taking together). Thus the present status of research infact on Arunachal Pradesh is very few and they hardly provide any insight into the socio-political process and behaviour of the people.

## Priority Areas for Future Research

As seen from the foregoing discussion Arunachal Pradesh is virtually a virgin area in as far as socio-political researchers are concerned. Researches on any area are, therefore, equally important. Besides, research priorities depend on the personality and interest of the researcher and, therefore, it differs from researcher to researcher. However, in view of the constraints of resources, both financial and otherwise and a very few number of scholars coming forward to undertake research on socio-political aspects in Arunachal Pradesh, there is need to pin point a few priority areas in order to fruitfully use the energy and resources of the researchers in the coming years. They may be regarded as thrust areas under each of which there could be several specific topics or projects. Further, the research projects should be socially relevant and thus, should have an "applied" orientation so that it can provide a better understanding of the process of socio-economic and political development and transformation taking place in the state and can help formulation of better strategies for speedier development of the state. This is not to underplay the need for basic research or theory generation. Any good piece of research helps the theory building, but the basic aim of political science research in the state should be information generation and orientation of outlook having relevance to desirable social change and improvement of the quality of life of the people of the state. Keeping these consideration in view; the following thrust areas may be identified for research in the 21st century.

### *Data Generation*

Every researcher in Arunachal Pradesh in the area of Arunachal Pradesh, faces difficulty in getting enough data for analysing the nature and pattern of a social problem. Enough studies for information generation, therefore, should be undertaken in Arunachal Pradesh. This is true not only in Political Science but all other social sciences. The available government or agency provided data are often not so reliable and unreliable data cannot be used in any good research. So scientifically generated research based data will help future researchers to carry out fruitful studies for understanding socio-political problems.

### *Social Change and Development Studies*

Recently a spurt of developmental activities have taken place in Arunachal Pradesh in all walks of life. Evaluative and desirability studies of these developments will go a long way in planning future strategies of development and in identifying their constraints. The impact of these developments on the tribal people of the state and their perception of these developments should be an important sub-area of this thrust area for research. As in case of data generation, this too is common to all social science disciplines.

### *Studies Relating to Traditional Socio-Political Institution*

All the tribes of Arunachal Pradesh have traditional socio-political institutions and until recently they regulated all aspects of life in the villages. Under the impact of modernisation many of them are in the wane in their importance. They have their own positive potentialities for organised life in the village. Research studies should be undertaken to identify these elements and to understand the positive aspects of these institutions. The age-old customary laws should be recorded and studied and their positive aspects identified.

### *Population Dynamics and Social Demography*

Population dynamics and social demography had great impact on social, cultural, economic and religious fronts and therefore, greatly influence political behaviour of the people. In view of the existence of a large number of tribes with social, cultural, and linguistic differences and also in view of their exposure to each other as well as to the outsiders in a scale never occurred before, this ought to be an important thrust area for research for social science scholars in future. This should also include the impact of movement of population, although still in a very small scale, from one areas to another and from outside the state.

*Ethnicity, Inter-community Relation: Regionalism and Social Movements*

Since, in recent years ethnicity, regionalism and social movement have become a dominant political denominator in the North-Eastern Region, it is bound to have its own impact on Arunachal Pradesh. Besides, inter community relationship is bound to be an important factor in shaping the socio-economic behaviour of the people in Arunachal Pradesh. Therefore, efforts should be made to understand these dynamics in relation to political behaviour in the state.

*Studies Relating to Processes of National Integration and Nation Building*

This can be another thrust area for research in Arunachal Pradesh. Research proposals can be developed focusing on proper identification of linkage between the people of the state and the rest of the country. Inter-dependence between the state and the rest of the North-Eastern Region and the country can be properly explored and assessed. Historical and cultural ties between the people of the state and rest of the country also may be understood in its proper perspective, which will provide a greater understanding of the state and nation building process taking in the state.

In addition to these, individual researchers may identify other important areas such as women studies, studies relating to environmental problem's, ecosystem, planning etc., having bearing on political and social life in the area.

## NOTES AND REFERENCES

1. B. Pakem, "Social responsibility of investigators and Researchers studying social, economic and political problem in N.E. Region" *Journal of NEICSSR*, October 1990.

CHAPTER 4

# Research Priorities in Economics

*N.C. Roy*

That economic research generates new knowledge of economics and raises the level of cognition of a society is very well-known, and so it sounds rather hackneyed. Not that the generation of pure theoretical knowledge alone provides raison d' etre of economic research, rather the variety of practical uses to which the product of economic research is put underlines the main rationale of economic research. Hardly any government economic policy can prove successful in modern times unless it is formulated on the basis of a reliable information of the economy, and it is research which can provide policy-required information about the economy. In the absence of research-generated systematic information, the trial and error method is adopted in policy formulation, and thus expensive adhocism becomes the norm, leading to the sub-optimal policy outcome. It is not the government alone which requires and uses the product of economic research, individuals, firms, institutions also utilize the output of economic research in their decision making.

Ever since the construction of an empirical macro-economic model of Netherlands economy by Tinbergen in 1936 to study the effects of certain measures of economic policy, like exchange rate change, import restrictions, reduction in government expenditure, etc., the macro-economic models of the developed countries have proliferated and it has been the normal practice of the government in the developed countries to utilize and preparation. It is because of these problems that in the preliterate societies in general, economic research has not advanced much; rather soft type of research such as the anthropological one has proceeded the economic research. The anthropologists can rush where the economists fear to tread. The anthropologists usual strategy of data collection is participant observation and the basic approach is holistic—the study of all aspects of man. The economic approach is not holistic and participant observation is too time consuming and expensive to be appealing to the economists.

However, economic research cannot avoid the method of participant observation, this method when suitably modified appears to be the only feasible method to collect accurate information from the rural areas.

## IV

In the presence of so many constraints that confront the economic research in Arunachal Pradesh, it is desirable that the areas of research be well-defined and priorities properly set out. Specially, the scarcity of resources—both human and materials must be kept in consideration while charting out the course of research. A modest beginning can be made with the applied research, more specifically with the policy research. Cost-wise this appears feasible and the output of the research will be directly useful to the government.

In the priority scale, therefore, the study of government economic policy can be assigned the first position. The policy research would provide the estimation of the output generated by the government's policy input, pinpoint the pitfalls in the operation of the policy and suggest by objective analysis the possible improvement. Unless the government's economic policy is evaluated by an independent research institution on the basis of primary information collected from the supposed beneficiaries of the particular policy measures, a correct picture of the policy impact can not emerge. The evaluation of government policy by an organ of the government is likely to give a biased picture, so the policy research by an independent research body is a *sine qua-non*. The policy research is suggested not only because it is cost effective and useful to the government but also because the policy research is simple having well defined objective and frame of reference which make it easy to execute.

Of the government's economic policy set, an important policy sub-set is one that concerns with removal of poverty and creation of productive employment. The Integrated Rural Development Programme (IRDP) is such a programme launched to remove poverty. Elsewhere in the country a number of studies have been undertaken to estimate the impact of the programme and suggest possible measures for the improved operation of the same. In Arunachal Pradesh the operation of IRDP and different employment generation schemes can be studied to gauge their impact, and suggestion for possible improvement can be made.

The financial side of the government's economic policy is looked after by credit policy. The credit policy is framed by the IRDP. However, the actual operation of the credit policy is shaped at least partly by the state government and local bodies. The rural target groups for credit are determined by the panchayat. The level of operation of the financial institution gives a good image of the growth of income, the expansion of the commercial sector etc. The productivity of credit is a good measure of the productivity of capital. So, the study of the productivity effect of credit can give a good picture of the possibility of the expansion of banking and financial services and the growth of the commercial and industrial sectors. A study of the growth of banking habit of the people, the productivity of bank credit, the sources of credit, especially in the rural areas, are some of the important areas which appear promising in research.

Closely related with government's economic policy is the population policy. The study of population policy is of paramount importance. India is the first country in the world to introduce family welfare programme at the government level. In Arunachal Pradesh the family welfare programme has been running for a long time. Elsewhere, the family welfare programme and its impact upon the fertility have been studied intensively. In Arunachal Pradesh similar studies can shed light upon the operation of the programme and its impact.

On completion of the first stage of research which is concerned with the policy evaluation being directed to estimate the impact of the existing or past policies and programmes concerned with the removal of poverty and creation of employment, expansion of banking and financial services and population control, the next step of research should be concerned with the study of the current economic status of the population, their employment status, their mobility through space and time and the working of the industrial and agricultural sectors. In the study of current economic status, the information which are of utmost importance are the level and sources of family income, the pattern of family expenditure and the level and mode of saving. These information give saving ratio, an important economic parameter and the poverty ratio, the proportion of families (population) living below the poverty line which is a very important policy variable. The estimation of family income will make it possible to compare the micro level income data with the macro level (The central statistical organisation (CSO) estimates and publishes regularly Arunachal's income statistics).

The study of poverty should get proper stress at this stage. Associated with poverty are unemployment and under employment. The creation of productive employment—including the productive self-employment—is the only way to overcome poverty. Employment creation would necessitate the expansion of industry including the traditional handicrafts and at this stage the feasibility of establishment of large scale industry and some mechanization of agriculture should receive due attention. The social cost benefit analysis should be applied to make decision as to the desirability or agricultural mechanization and industrial expansion.

In Arunachal Pradesh the population growth rate is high, much higher than the national growth rate. In the eighties national population growth rate was 2.4 percent per annum while Arunachalee growth rate was 3.6 percent per annum (provisional population census 1991). This high growth in Arunachal Pradesh is not the natural growth, it is due to high rate of immigration. The launch of various development programmes has necessitated the employment of workers from outside the state. The growth of township, expansion of trade commerce and industry have tended to accelerate the process of immigration. However, the migration from outside the state is not permanent, it is transitory; the migrants can not settle here permanently, so they can not be said to add to the population and create population problem. What remains problematic is the intrastate migration and urbanization. The study of population growth, urbanization, intrastate migration, etc. should receive due attention in view of the problem they are likely to create in future.

## V

Once sufficient research output has been produced through applied research, it would be possible to generalize and create a new conceptual framework to capture the specific economic situation of this state. The construction of economic theory pre-supposes the existence of a whole body of social-cultural institutions. Different institutional arrangement leads to a different configuration of economic relations and this tends to shape a different theoretical framework. So, there are capitalist economics and socialist economics. Similarly, Arunachalee economy would necessitate the development of hill or tribal economics and this will be possible only when applied research has reached some maturity. The generalization and abstraction require sufficient observations; only after a good build-up of output by applied research the theory construction can be undertaken and a synthesis between theoretical and applied aspects made. Here some caution is to be exercised. The Arunachalee economy is not static; here rapid economic changes are taking place, the process of urbanization has intensified. The urbanization, industrialization and commercialization of production are likely to set in motion the process of detribalization and dilute the traditional economic relations. So when sufficient empirical findings will be available, Arunachalee economy may pass into a modern economy, leaving far behind the traditionalism and rendering irrelevant the construction of tribal economics.

## VI

To conclude, we are to recapitulate that the successful start of systematic research in Arunachal Pradesh is the problem; once some new ground is cut, the research here like elsewhere will be a self-sustaining process. The age of information has come. Information is an important development input and valued in the literate society; the output of research is information. Initially in Arunachal Pradesh, the government will remain the primary and academics the secondary consumers of the output of research. With the growth of literacy, urbanization, and industrialization the demand for research will increase and in due course the demand will settle the problem of prioritization of research.

## NOTES

1. To give just a few examples, game theory developed by Von-Neumann and Morgenstein to explain strategic economic behaviour has found fertile applications not only in political science and sociology but also in military science and international relations *i.e.* it has been used to explain every type of strategic human behaviour. Similarly, human capital model and capital asset pricing model have found applications beyond economics. Perhaps George Stigler, the Noble Laureate economist has rightly called economics the "Imperial science".
2. Modern economics is concerned with the problems of industrial economics—the economics where agriculture has also been industrialized. Economics, as it is, can hardly study the economic problems of a pre-industrial society, where barter is the rule, differentiation is not readily observable and there is all pervading traditionalism in production, exchange and distribution.
3. Research activity is not created in a vacuum only when the output of research is demanded by someone, the research activity comes into being. In Arunachal Pradesh, no big industry has yet come up, the market is small, so is the commercial sector. Under the circumstances, research initiative is not likely to come from the industrialists. The

only demander—apart from the research institutions of the country—of the research output is the government, both the state and the central, and this calls for the prioritization of government policy related research.

## REFERENCE

Barten A.P., *Macroeconomic model construction,* Cabay, Leuven, 1981.

*Census of India,* 1991

Central Bureau of Statistics, National Accounts Statistics different issues.

Nerlove, M., "A Tabular Survey of macro-econometric models", *International Economic Review,* 7 (1966).

CHAPTER 5

# Research Priorities in Political Science

*S.N. Ali*

Political Science studies the interactions that shape institutions, processes and procedures through which authoritative allocations of goods and services are made in a given society. In other words it throws light on the modalities of shaping and sharing of power and seeks answer on who gets what when and how. Besides analysis of problems and phenomena it also prescribes policies for progressive resolution of conflicts so as to effect integration and adaptation in the entire system. In contrast to this behavioural paradigm, Marxist theory investigates the role of political power in relation to social classes and exposes its partisan role in the framework of dominant/subordinate class relations in a given mode of production. While Behaviouralists overrate the neutrality of the system, Marxists tend to underestimate its relative autónomy, given the complex nature of class configurations in the emerging modern societies. Between these two contrasting ideological extremes, research remains the only scientific means to ascertain the nature of specific aspects of political reality.

Politics, of late, has become all pervasive regulating all aspects of societal, national and international life from cradle to grave. No branch of human endeavour, today, remains uninformed and unguided by the values, norms and procedures defined by politics. War and peace, conduct of international relations, policies on history, economics, science, art, literature, language, religion and culture, in short, in every aspect of creativity and change, politics retains a major say. Rajni Kothari rightly observes that if modernisation is the general phenomenon in our times, then politicisation is its central tendency. May be Aristotle was right to hold it as a Master Science.

Despite growing importance of the discipline at a global scale, political science research in India not to speak of Arunachal is still at its infancy. Very little headway, has been made, indeed to evaluate and understand the role of power in its multifarious dimensions in this country. Certainly the constraints of research are many: continental size; vast population; perplexing diversities; peculiar colonial legacies; historical distortions; co-existence of multiple modes of production; lack of adequate institutional, financial, professional support for research; absence of co-ordination and net working among research institutions, problems of reference and data collection; non-cooperation by respondents; sabotage by vested interests; and above all, lack of necessary motivation and commitment on the part of intellectuals are just to mention a few of such problems. The result is naturally disastrous, forfeiting the rights of political scientists to intervene in any major crisis in any meaningful sense.

Survey of research in Arunachal Pradesh leads to the irresistible conclusion that its two prominent sources are British administrator cum anthropologists and the government. Most of the work done by the Research Department, Government of Arunachal Pradesh have social-anthropological overtones. A few books written on the state generally duplicate British accounts, census findings and official laws and enactments from time to time. Scanty works of research nature having relevance to political science are too micro in perspective and occupy very little of the total political space in terms of variety and time. A number of such research articles available till date in various books and journals have not made much difference either.

Hence, it may not sound exaggerated to say that Arunachal offers a virgin ground in terms of research possibilities in political science. In the light of reported vacuum, fixing priorities becomes all the more important to make a reasonable beginning with the limited resources available for the purpose.

May I then, suggest the following themes as priority areas for the 21st century.

*i) Nation-Building, State-Building and Processes of National Integration*

The island of peace, that is Arunachal is a peculiar exception in the trouble-torn, violent North-Eastern Region. The peaceful transition from primitive, colonial and post-colonial reorganisations into a full-fledge state offers a unique case of nation-building, state-building which preemted strains that adversely affect the processes of national integration. Besides, Arunachal-Building itself has emerged as a precious by-product of these processes wielding together diverse races and cultures into a single polity. All these offer an exciting opportunity for a researcher to study the interactions of endogenous and exogenous factors, individuals, groups and institutions, governmental and non-governmental organisations that have made possible such peaceful transition. The study will also highlight the defects/weaknesses, if any, in these processes so as to suggest possible policy inputs to plug the loopholes in them.

*ii) Political Leadership/Political Elites*

Pandit Jawaharlal Nehru, Verrier Elwin, Sir Akbar Ali Hydari, Nari Rustomji and others who shaped the destiny of Arunachal after Independence, had stressed the development of local leadership among the tribes so that government could be carried on under later's active participation and supervision. This goal seems to have largely been achieved as we see today, local leaders play prominent roles at various levels—panchayats, assemblies, ministries, administration and parliaments. It is time now that one investigates the processes of recruitment of political leaders, their orientation and role performance in various sphere of life. This will throw light on the level of cohesion and conflict, harmony and dissent among themselves and the nature of their linkages as well as involvement with the masses. Since political leadership constitutes the inchpin of North-Eastern tribal societies, this kind of study will focus on the role and activities of chief agents of development and modernisation in their respective societies. Obviously this will also explain the terms of interactions and means of mobilization through which the leaders compete for power and position.

*iii) Political Parties and Political Development*

Political development both as a concept and process remains a problematic in the theoretical plane. Yet its utility in measuring the nature and degree of transition in the tradition-modernity continuum cannot be ignored. Variables like institutionalization, role differentiation, democratization and secularization, have proved immensely beneficial in observing trends and direction of political change in different societies. Political parties perform several functions—political education, recruitment and training of leadership, political mobilization, elections, interest articulation and aggregation and as such define the broad processes of shaping and sharing of power that characterize the nature and level of political development. In Arunachal too, political parties have played a crucial role in internalizing the concepts of political authority, political regime and political community in a complex, heterogeneous society. Thus, the nature of party system that is evolving, its merits and demerits, contributions and failures in terms of effecting a proper course of political development is bound to attract the attention of researchers in the field.

*iv) Politics, Buraucracy, and Social Change*

Social change in a broad context implies all aspects of change—social, economic, political, cultural, psychological etc. which affect the individual and group values and behaviour. People of Arunachal remained stagnant for centuries for geographical, topographical and historical reasons. At the time they became the citizens of free India, there was hardly any awareness among them about the philosophy of Indian constitution or the institutions of modern governments. In short span of forty years people have made miraculous progress in every field of modern activity. In this process, role of politics and bureaucracy needs no emphasis. Yet there are reports that all is not well in the realm of social change. Aberrations like inter-regional disparities, inter-community inequalities, emerging hierarchy of status and income, large scale erosion of social ethos and cultural traditions, crash materialism and opportunism leading to various form of corruption, etc. tend to threaten the very peace in this island of peace. Research into role of political leadership and bureaucratic machinery may provide more insight about how and why such aberrations appear and what can be done for their redressal.

*v) Panchayati Raj and Rural Development*

The concept of Panchayati Raj is a product of the feeling that popular participation in matters of local administration and development will produce better results in every sphere. It may be mentioned that integration of diverse people began in a political sense after the introduction of Panchayati Raj and Apex Council by the administration. While Panchayati Raj institutions gradually eroded the influence of traditional authorities, the modern representatives like legislator, council of ministers, etc., tend to overshadow the panchayat leaders. The recent move for financial/administrative devolution of power to the grassroots holds new promises for the resurgence of these institutions. By far, it remains to be evaluated how much success these institutions have achieved in implementing programmes on rural development, free from partisan influences of dominant classes and often baneful interferences by political parties. Thus organisation, election, functions, finances, autonomy, administrative and political patronage, and many such issues need assessment in order to know as to how much potential there exists in Arunachal to carry democracy and development to the grass roots.

## Conclusion

The broad themes suggested above may be subdivided into multiple sub-themes in tune with specificity and demands of micro-research. The absence of institutional support for research calls for immediate commencement of research programmes in the only University of the state. Besides, setting up of some research institutes publications of journals and more intimate and effective interaction of local scholars with the regional and national centres for the purpose may also go a long way in filling up the void of Research in the state.

CHAPTER 6

# Priorities in Historical Research

*Tamo Mibang*

The study of history of the Arunachal tribes with distinct language and culture is a fascinating subject but not a simple task as the research for and collection of data, documents etc., the first part of the historian's craft, has its limitation and problems in Arunachal.

The popular belief of the people is that their history is mingled in the mist of tradition and mythology. So, while dealing with the origin and migrations of the people, we mainly rely on historical tradition—Kebang/Abe of the Adis, hymns of the Miris/Nibus, legends and folklore, etc., of the various tribes. In Adi, a gifted orator is called 'Kebang' who traces the origin and migration of the people of the central zone from Uli, Usha, Kumting in Tibet in a poetic language. The Apatanis, Nishings, Tagins also trace their history from the north and most of the Tribes of eastern zone from South-East Asia.

A Kebang, normally gives his discourse in an extraordinary open gathering. In olden times, with his oratory power, he could provoke the whole community to raise arms against their enemy or he could convince them in sympathetic tone to give up their plan for battle. The discourse is to be tape recorded first by researchers and then translated and finally written it.

Here, the main problem of the researchers is the finding out of such an appropriate occasion or gathering. Because such occasion is very rare. So, we tried this in 1982 at Pasighat club where Mr. Matpang, Tamuk of Mongku and Mr. Ogom Dai of Balek Village were invited to deliver Kebang, and at Kiyit Village in 1987 where Mr. Taluk Tamuk of Pasighat, Mr. A. Megu of Kiyit, and Mr. N. Mitkong of Pasighat participated and again at Boleng in 1989 where Mr. Mutnyi Komut of Rumgong with his discourse completely silenced the audience.

Likewise, the hymns of the Miris/Nibus of Adis, Apatanis, Nishings and Tagins. They not only invoke various gods, goddesses and evil-spirits to free the soul of the ailing person but also in their hymns trace the entire genealogies of the family or of the community. During festival days like Mopin, Solung, Dree, Nyokum etc., they trace the whole cultural life of the people in a most classical poetic language which we ordinary people hardly understand. Here, the researchers are to observe the events personally with necessary equipments for recording and photography.

Myths, legends and folklore etc., are also very important for reconstructing the social history of the people. In Arunachal, there are hundreds of folktales and folklore among the various tribes. To collect these, researchers are to do an extensive field work in a selected compact area to interview some aged-persons and story tellers. However, to do this, one has to know the language of the people or a personal interpreter is a must. Many research scholars face this problem everywhere. Some scholars like Verrier Elwin and Sachin Roy have done their works with the help of good interpreters, and so their works appear to be original with beauty.

In addition to this, one is to appreciate difficult terrain and communication problems. Interior areas are still inaccessible and so even local Arunachal officials are not willing to go to those areas on posting. Resolute will and determination can alone surmount these problems.

Kabang, an ornamental cultural literature of the Adis, deals with the mythology on the creation of the universe and mankind. Mr. Talom Rukbo of Pasighat has done some important works on this. This are: *Sedi—Melo Kelang Among Talling Abang, Ekop Abang, Agam Bedang Abang, Limir Sobo* etc. All are in Adi language. Only translation into other languages is awaited. These is no compulsion that one must write in English. One can write in any Indian language. Then history as well as local language will be preserved and developed. Leave the translation part to other interested scholars.

Study of place names of Arunachal is also important. Every, place has its original name which is associated with historical events. Researchers are to do an extensive fieldwork on this. But, it is seen that some administrators, planners are distorting the historical names of various places. For instance Gyakar Sinyi as Ganga Lake, Daudi as Vijayanagar, Sidhi as Gandhigram and so on. Reasons are best known to themselves, but this certainly annoys the local indigenous people. However, the Directorate of Research, Arunachal Pradesh, with various research wings, may like to answer to this query. It is true, that this Directorate have already published hundreds of works on Arunachal, yet we expect some more genuine works from them in days to come.

We admit that the traditional way of life of our people, hardly leaves any trace, to give chronological clues to researchers. Therefore, we shall have to accept the available oral records to write the history of Arunachal as told by the people themselves. To do this due financial incentive to researchers is the first requisite.

The Tibetan literature preserved in the monastery consists of the canonical scriptures and the commentaries. There are other records also such as account books, receipts, agreements, sanads and *parwanas*. They are valuable historical sources. In this connection, mention may be made of Aitchison's *A collection of Treaties, Enactment and Sanads Relating to India and the Neighbouring Countries* (in 4 volumes) 1931, reprinted 1973 (Germany). The Tai literature of the Khamtis is also rich. There are works on law, social and political conditions. Local Monpa, Sherdukpen and Khamti scholars can explore more records. Appointment of Local scholars as D.R.D., A.R.O. and L.O. to their respective places is perhaps the right approach of the Directorate of Research, Arunachal Pradesh and will generate more research literature.

Some Assamese Buranjis like Harakanta Baruah's *Assam Buranji* (ed.) by S.K. Bhuyan; *Kamrupa Buranji*; *A History of Assam—Mughal Conflict* (ed.) by S.K, Buyan; Shihabuddin Talishs work *Tarikh-i-Assam* also called as *Fathiyya-i-I briyya* (1662–63). *North-East Frontier of Bengal* by Alexander